T0194568

Chapter

11

A Bankruptcy Personal Reorganization

Ruth DiDomenico

WESTBOW
PRESS®
A DIVISION OF THOMAS NELSON
& ZONDERVAN

Copyright © 2019 Ruth DiDomenico.

All rights reserved. No part of this book may be used or reproduced by any means, graphic, electronic, or mechanical, including photocopying, recording, taping or by any information storage retrieval system without the written permission of the author except in the case of brief quotations embodied in critical articles and reviews.

This book is a work of non-fiction. Unless otherwise noted, the author and the publisher make no explicit guarantees as to the accuracy of the information contained in this book and in some cases, names of people and places have been altered to protect their privacy.

WestBow Press books may be ordered through booksellers or by contacting:

WestBow Press
A Division of Thomas Nelson & Zondervan
1663 Liberty Drive
Bloomington, IN 47403
www.westbowpress.com
1 (866) 928-1240

Because of the dynamic nature of the Internet, any web addresses or links contained in this book may have changed since publication and may no longer be valid. The views expressed in this work are solely those of the author and do not necessarily reflect the views of the publisher, and the publisher hereby disclaims any responsibility for them.

Any people depicted in stock imagery provided by Getty Images are models, and such images are being used for illustrative purposes only.
Certain stock imagery © Getty Images.

ISBN: 978-1-9736-4891-8 (sc)
ISBN: 978-1-9736-4892-5 (e)

Print information available on the last page.

WestBow Press rev. date: 1/17/2019

Contents

Acknowledgments

I am so grateful to my friend Joyce Scales for her computer expertise and the generous expenditures of her time in this project. Thanks also to my neighbor Mark Moore for his internet expertise contribution. Thanks to Dr. Lucienne Lanson for her encouragement, suggestions, and recommendations for publishing on the manuscript. Thanks to Isaac Rojas from Live Oaks Church tech staff for his technical contributions. Thanks to Frankie Brassard for her time in editing this manuscript and suggestions for improvement. Thanks to my supportive family who are my bedrocks in surviving difficult times.

Introduction to Chapter 11

Chapter 11 in legal terms is a "business bankruptcy reorganization plan". My Chapter 11 is a "personal bankruptcy reorganization plan". It began at the death of my husband of 62 years. All of life changed from this day forward. I felt HIS unmistakable presence during one full week of Lou's death. At first, I was only aware of changes, then a series of circumstances, and finally an appreciation, trust, and submission to HIS guidance. In one week, I became a different person, doing different things in a different way.

In this book, the first 10 chapters briefly preface the early years during the great depression, followed by teenage foibles, college years, first job, military years, marriage and family, all referenced from a book I had written called Notes from a Full House.

When Lou and I moved to The Villages, a retirement community, we were happily enjoying the fruits of our labors when overnight, life changed. Surprisingly this whole new life puts all the life before into a new perspective and the path after described in Chapter 11 holds the most profound joy I have ever experienced. At 90 years of age I look forward to each day to more of the same and embrace each day as a blessing and an opportunity for more. Too bad I had to be so old to find the keys to a purpose driven life and the peace that being a Christian brings.

One

1929

1929 was the year the great depression began in the United States that lasted decades before financial sanity returned to the average family. I was born into a family that had two older boys which were already a burden in those days, but I was female and that made my arrival that much more of a burden. My family lived in a small house with one bathroom with my father's two sisters and their families containing another four children. Only one of the men had a job, that of a policeman. Obtaining enough food for this group was a big problem. In those days, when one was successful in obtaining a job, keeping this job was a top priority, no matter the price paid to keep it.

My first memories were that of moving into a big house that housed my father's mother and father. They were to live on the upper floors along with their youngest daughter who was then in her early 20's. Because my brothers shared one of the 2 bedrooms downstairs, I was assigned upstairs with my aunt Peg. She was less than delighted to share her space with me just because I wet the bed and threw up a lot.

I thought aunt Peg was beautiful and I loved to watch her get ready to go out on her dates with various boyfriends. I made a point of greeting them all and telling them all about how popular she was. The house had a parlor room where she greeted her friends and many times entertained them. No one had any money to go anywhere. This room had a glass transom on top of the folding doors where you could see into the room from the stairway just outside. I sold access for my neighbors for a penny each for as long as they were quiet enough. This did not make me any more charming to her.

Grandma and Grandpa had been wealthy business owners, farmers, and land owners in Kentucky before the depression, but moved the family to Detroit where Henry Ford started mass producing automobiles that were replacing the horse and buggy and there were more jobs available. Grandpa finally got a job as a streetcar conductor. One of the assets was all the stuff he brought home from the things people left on the streetcar. My brother played the clarinet, and I payed the trumpet. It helped push my buck teeth back in place.

He was never good at fixing stuff like the furnace. He would go down to shake the coals and get it stuck, then go out to find some parts and not come back home for 3 days or so while we all froze. He would drink to calm his nerves, and I saw Grandma blow her nose into her apron a lot during these times.

It was 1939 before the economy began to pick up when Germany attacked Poland and France starting World War 2. Japan struck Pearl Harbor in 1941 starting the need for defensive equipment and supplies. It was several years before we moved into our house in Dearborn, Michigan.

Two

School years

I was in the 5th grade when we moved to Dearborn into our own house. My brothers plus another brother addition had the upstairs and I had my own bedroom. I loved the school a block away from our house that provided a space for a summer recreation program that functioned admirably by the city of Dearborn. They provided a leader, playground equipment, tournaments and movies, watermelon fests, and amateur nights, etc. We had inter- playground baseball tournaments, swim opportunities to some schools etc. It was a perfect place to raise children and grand opportunities to spend fruitful summers.

My father was a farm boy from Kentucky and loved the fresh cantaloupes, fruit trees, fresh vegetables that included corn on the cob, potatoes, tomatoes that were ripe off the vines, green beans, etc. so he would shepherd us kids to work the fields in the summer and in the winter would bank the edges and fill it full of water for an ice skating rink that was a delight of the neighborhood children.

When it was time to go to junior high school, a friend and I would walk about a mile through the woods to school. This has been a lifelong friend who was in the grade ahead of mine. When it came time to go to college, she would sell me her used books, for we were taking the same major scholastically. Loved her used books for she was a good student and underlined all the important things in the book that were usually asked for on follow up exams.

The high school years were very rewarding. After school activities were more of a focus than the studying part of going to school. I played in all the tennis tournaments (and won most of them), played on the school softball team, volleyball, and basketball teams. I even had a steady boyfriend whose parents thought he should have a more presentable girlfriend. They wanted for him one who was not Catholic, was rich like they were, and could not throw a ball farther than John could. Being brought up in a family of boys in a neighborhood of more boys, I was more at home jumping from garage to garage, swinging from tree to tree and running bases that reading a book or painting my nails or primping my hair, but I did like John. Our dates were trail hikes and coon hunting, and long drives in his father's car that had a telephone in it when no one else had this. He taught me how to drive and other things.

I ended up editing the school newspaper and was president of the Girl's Athletic Association. On graduation day I was awarded the Dorothy Dickinson Smith trophy as the most outstanding athletic award but missed the Honor Society by a mile.

Three

Post Graduation

I was planning to be a women's gym teacher, as this seemed like the best job in the world. To do the things you loved to do and get paid for it sounded perfect. Our gym teacher advised me to apply to the Michigan State Normal College from which she had graduated and recommended it to me. I was all exited about doing this when my mother approached me and said, "You cannot go to college, it is more important that your brothers go than for you. We cannot afford to send you too, you will just get married and have babies while your brothers will need to support a family".

I could not accept this. I skipped school and hitch hiked up to Ypsilanti, where the school of my choice was located. I went into the Dean of Women's Office and said that I would like to come to this school, and what did I have to do to make this happen. She outlined the procedures. I told her that I was going to need a job. Dean Hill said, "Oh, freshmen cannot work. They need time to get oriented and adjusted first." I just stood there and finally said, "You know, I am really tired of people telling me that I cannot do something. I am going to come to this school, I am going to graduate from this school, and if you are going to help me, wonderful, but if you are not, just don't stand in the way".

Dean Hill just sat back in her chair and looked at me for a long time. She reached over for her phone, dialed a number, and said into the phone, "Mr. Brownrigg, I am sending over a freshman to interview, and she has my permission to work". Dean Hill not only got me a job in the College Union pouring juice at 6:00 AM but was responsible for getting me scholarships and other advantages all through the 4 college years. It was as if she had adopted me as a project, and I have always been grateful for her caring. I had multiple jobs through those years including being recreation director for a juvenile delinquent home, City of Dearborn recreation department summer camp, a resort hotel in Maine along with a job in the Ogunquit downtown area at night for extra money. One night I waited on Eleanor Roosevelt while she was visiting Faye Emerson, her son's new wife, who was in a play at the local theater. One summer I worked as a waterfront director for a riding camp for girls in New Hampshire. Essentially, I always found a job that included room and board as part of the package and did not come home for almost two years. I remember the second Christmas that I did come home. My Dad was passing out $10.00 bills to my brothers. He got to me and hesitated. I said just keep it, and he put it back in his pocket. At the time they were angry at me for being disobedient and I was angry and disappointed at being disregarded. Looking back, it was probably the best life preparation I could have had. I remember walking up the isle at my graduation. I felt empowered. If I could do this, I could do anything. I have never felt any other way. I have always felt that I can do this, whatever it is.

I ended up my senior year with a B average, president of the Women's Athletic Association, roomed with the President of the Women's League, living in the suite for elites on the corner of the first floor of the dorm, and first choice of any job that was offered because of the recommendations from the staff.

Four

First Job

In a job interview the superintendent of schools stressed that the person for this job would have to be special because the school building was under construction and the gym was not yet finished. There was no equipment and there would have to be a very creative and resilient person to do this job. I was fascinated with the thought and the challenge and accepted the job. I liked the superintendent and the challenge, and it seemed like a match. Arriving at the school, the construction was farther behind than they had anticipated. I shared a full functioning bus garage as my gym, no equipment, and a broom closet as an office.

The head of our department at Ypsilanti had a former student who was the president of the Women's Field Hockey Association. She arranged to have used equipment that was being replaced by new, donated to our school, and then threw in some volleyballs and basketballs. I stored the hockey sticks in the broom closet. One student had her father mow a local field and created some goal posts with netting. We put some hoops and a volleyball net at our end of the garage and we were in business.

Our new principle was of the variety of "let the little dears express themselves". In other words, there was utter chaos. I remember seeing a stack of lockers outside the bus garage that I could really use for supplies that I was gathering, some of which I bought with my own money. I saw the principal coming down the hall and I followed him, asking him if I could have the lockers. He ignored me and kept walking. I followed him pleading my case about how much better my program would be with this little bit of addition. I said, "all you have to say is, yes you can have the lockers". He turned to me and with gritted teeth he said, "yes, you can have the lockers". It was here that I learned that I had followed him into the men's bathroom.

I was so disciplined by the time I finished college that I did not fit into this mayhem. While sitting in an NEA meeting (National Education Association), I looked around at all the prune faces, listened to the liberal educational philosophy, and walked out thinking I do not belong here. Down the hall there was an Army recruiting station with a sign saying, "Free coffee and doughnuts". My first thought was that the price was right, so I dropped in and ate their doughnuts and drank their coffee. Here Captain Biddle explained about a new program the army was starting called physical therapy, and they were looking for college graduates with a BS degree who would join in getting our wounded warriors back to "line of duty yes", strengthening soldiers in place of lying around while healing and getting weaker. I was interested, especially the part about a free trip to Texas and training for a year for what sounded like an interesting job. Captain Biddle surprised me with a visit to my school with more information. After conferring with my college friend (who sold me her books that were underlined), we decided to sign up. Finishing the school year, I was elected as teacher of the year by the student body.

We got in my car and drove to Fort Sam Houston, Texas. We were scheduled to meet another young woman from Michigan in San Antonio who was also signing up. We planned to meet in Texas and the Alamo was the only landmark we all recognized. We set the date and time at 6:00 PM. What a surprise to find thousands of people milling around. Dwight Eisenhower was having a rally as part of his run for president of the United States. Amazingly we found her. It was here that I really fit, as I was already disciplined and totally fascinated with the medical training. I would study well into the night in unrelated subjects just because it was so interesting and then must spend the rest of the night doing what I was supposed to study. This was the first time I had ever really studied and was in love with the work. There were 50 men for every woman and these men at Fort Sam were getting ready to deploy to Korea. We almost felt it was our patriotic duty to be charming. What a bad time to rather be studying.

Spent 7 months in didactic training and then sent to the Letterman Army Hospital in San Francisco for the clinical training. San Francisco was at that time a very exciting place and the work was fascinating. We had the best training possible by some of the most dedicated and competent people. For example, we had an orthopedic surgeon as our anatomy instructor, cadavers for lab, busloads of amputees for bandaging, a psychiatrist who had been on the Bataan Death March for psychology of the ill and the handicapped, etc. These wounded warriors were proud of what they had done and were doing all they could to get well. What a shock it was to get out into the civilian world and find many that were more interested in not going back to work.

I was then assigned to Fitzsimmons Army Hospital in Denver, Colorado. One memorable day I remember standing in line in the front row watching the then President Eisenhower leave the hospital after his heart attack rehabilitation.

On my 27thbirthday, all the therapists in our clinic took me to the free beer night at the Officer's Club at the Lowrey Air Force Base. It was here that I met Louis DiDomenico. He was the one I eventually married and spent the next 62 years living the dream. Our dates were unusual. During those days, the military encouraged their pilots to fly on their spare time for increased efficiency. We would go out to the flight line and find a flight going out. We would petition for "permission to board" and when accepted which was often, we could fly to wherever they were going. Maybe it was to fly to San Francisco to dinner, or to Arizona for a football game, or any other destination that had a return flight. We could stay at the Officer's Clubs for a dollar a night per room. We spent a lot of time at the Greyhound Dog racing track. In graduate school my work required research and a dissertation. Lou was reassigned during these times to Alamogordo, New Mexico, the experimental guided missile base as an aerospace engineer with a lot of pilots. It was here that he learned to fly and bought a single engine Cessna airplane. When his pilot friends came through Denver, many times they would stop to pick me up (qualified as an active reserve officer) to fly with them to Alamogordo where I would stay at the Officer's club for $1.00 per night. I would research and write my thesis during the day, and dine and dance at night, then wait for a ride back when available, usually less than a week. The big adventure was flying with Lou in his new airplane with his brand-new flying license in hand. We were taking this maiden flight from Denver Colorado to Ohio and Michigan where we were going to announce our engagement to our parents.

ep flying high Lou

Lou learned to fly in the New Mexico mountains and usually stayed above 10,000 feet altitude to miss the peaks. In the flat lands of mid America, that is usually where the clouds are located. It is easy to get disoriented without reference. A few times I asked if the altimeter circling meant anything. Many times, we flew over the towns below to catch the name of the town by the letters on the water towers, so we knew where we were. There are memories of looking for an airport when we were running out of fuel. I remember pushing the plane up to the pumps by hand from the runway because we did not have enough fuel to motor up. These were indeed exciting times and we were glad to be still alive at the end of that trip. We were planning to fly to Cleveland to meet Lou's parents first but changed our minds when we flew over the water tower and the letters spelled out "DETROIT", so we decided to meet my parents first.

Five

Marriage and Family

Post Military, Lou secured a job as an aerospace engineer at the Boeing Airplane Company in Seattle, Washington. I utilized the GI Bill that allowed returning veterans to go to any school of their choice with paid tuition, books, and $100.00 a month. This was and is a wonderful "Thank you for your service" gift that gave the service men and women an opportunity to prepare themselves for an upgraded future and for their further contribution to a better USA. Upon my graduation from the University of Colorado, we got married in Michigan and took several weeks leisurely driving his new car across the country and landed happily in Seattle to settle into this new life.

We arrived late December in the middle of the academic first quarter, but having nothing else to do, I drove up to the University of Washington and walked into the President's office. I told him that I realized it was an unusual time of year to be looking for a job, but I was looking for whatever information I should be gathering to qualify in the future. He questioned me about my qualifications and then handed me his card with the names of the head of the school of nursing and the head of the Women's Athletic Department. I first went to the Athletic Department and walked up to the desk and said that I had just graduated with a master's degree in physical therapy from the University of Colorado. A woman's voice down the halls calls out and says, "who has a master's degree in physical therapy?" A physical therapy program was just being initiated at UW, and they had a preliminary pre-physical therapy program going on. One faculty member had gotten pregnant and was too ill to attend her classes for weeks. By the end of the following week, I had an offer to teach primarily health education classes, pre-physical therapy mentoring counselor, beginning swimming, and ski coach at double the salary I had ever made. I could not believe my good fortune. I spent the remainder of that year and the next one teaching before getting into the baby making business and had 4 children in the next 4 years. I needed to make room for a younger and less fertile female.

We bought 10 acres of waterfront property on Vashon Island where we planned to build our dream home. It has an outstanding view of Clovis passage and Lou's brother was an architect who designed a home for us that would take advantage the view. The property had two old cabins that had been vacant for several years and a well that needed "a little fixing". We had been renting a house from a "lady" who had a lover in Alaska. Things went badly for her and she arrived in the middle of the night demanding that we vacate immediately. She caused a big loud scene out on the street attracting the police department and resulting in Lou, the baby Eric, and the pregnant Ruth putting all our belongings into the little Fiat and taking off for our cabin in the woods on Vashon Island. It is here that we learned that the ferries stop running at midnight. Long story short, it was a bad night and not having any heat, light, gas, or water once we did arrive became more interesting. We secured a well driller who concluded that the pump at the bottom of the 200 ft well needed to be replaced. He hauled up the pipes and replaced the pump. He began to reinstall. I was standing there watching when he put on another link. He had not secured the last link firmly enough and it separated, smashing the 100 feet of pipe and the new pump that was attached. He looked down the hole, mumbled something, then put his tools back in his truck and drove off and was very hard to find after that. We found another driller who charged $250/ hr. to dredge for and replace the now broken pump and all pipes. At least we had water.

People on the Island are different. Vashon is where the book "The egg and I" was written and the follow up television series "Mom and Pa Kettle" originated. The neighbor who lived close to our well was friendly to us, but sad to see life changing. She and her husband had not been off the island for 7 years. She said that things were just getting too crowded for them. She added that she saw 2 cars go by yesterday and held up 2 fingers to make sure that I got the picture. Another neighbor came by and welcomed us and said that we could borrow their cat any time we wanted. I finally figured out that she meant her "caterpillar tractor". We made arrangements to have a man come and clean out one of the cabins. Weeks went by and he never showed up. When asked why he did not do what we had agreed upon, he answered, "well you don't' ask one day and we come out the next, you know". Most people on the Island live by their own rules, like getting a driver's license or not. A couple of times a year the State Police make an unannounced visit to issue fines on unlicensed drivers. The ferry crew will call ahead and issue a warning to their friend and neighbors of police presence. The phones would ring off the hook and suddenly the road traffic disappeared until the "all clear" signal went out. Don't know if that is still an issue, but in the old days, that is the way it was.

We kind of lived in one cabin while we cleared out and were fixing up the other cabin to live-in while we built our house. We bought plaster board and spackle and I set to work lining the walls. I would put Eric in the playpen, hammer and nail boards and then spackle. Wanting to do a really good job, I put on a LOT of spackle. When it all dried, the big lumps stood out and it was obvious that this needed to be sanded to make it flush to paint. Eric was just learning to stand. He would pull himself up, get tired and cry out for help. I would climb down from the ladder, sit him down, and then climb back to work to have the scene repeat itself. When I put him on a blanket on the floor, he got his exercise by following ants and try to catch them, and I think he cut some teeth on number 2 sandpaper. Going back and forth in the rain after spackle dusting was also an interesting experience. All our clothes and hair were stiff when they dried.

With the new baby due to arrive any day, Lou was working a lot of overtime and the ferries stopped working at midnight. We moved into a new house in the city. What a joy it was to have running water, a washing machine, flush toilets, and an actual super market where you could buy diapers and fresh food and all the things that real people use in their daily lives.

Six

Maturtion

Lou had always wanted to have his own business. He was focused on making sure that all his growing family of one son and two daughters now had the opportunity for the best education to prepare them to develop all their talents for a happy future. We got into the Norge Coin Operated dry cleaning business.

Stephen Gregory was born on June 5. It was a busy day. Working at the store was an easier job than taking care of the other 3. I opted to work until 5:00 PM. I checked into the hospital at 6:00, started into hard labor at 7:00 and delivered at 10:50 PM. Lou was there for the entire delivery as with the other 3 deliveries. It was the easiest delivery of the group. We checked out of the hospital the next morning and into the Hilton Inn. It was a wonderful experience with the plush surroundings and the room service. I had planned to breast feed Steve but had one difficulty. He was a lusty little fellow and got hungry before my milk came in. I ran out of Enfamil and sugar water and nothing was open in the middle of the night. I listened to him cry, and rocking did not console him, so I crushed up a banana and fed it to him. He ate it happily and went back to sleep for several hours. By the time he awoke, my milk was flowing. Lou came after work, we would order dinner from room service. They would roll in an oven with a table cloth on it and serve prime rib with fresh vegetables. Beats hospital watery soup and meat loaf. The following nights Lou would bring all the kids into the room, we would order hamburgers and French fries, sit around and watch television. Everybody would get to love and hold the new baby. One child got to stay all night with Mom and baby. The following day, I would go down to the swimming pool and dangle my feet and sit on the beach chairs in the sun with my new baby. It was a fun time for all.

It all got started when I checked into deliveries ahead of time because I did not want to be held up at the front desk when it was time. The lady at the desk says to me, "that will be $300.00". I answer, "I am only going to be staying for 3 days". She laughs loudly, tells all the workers around her about my ignorance, and says with a smile still on her face, "Lady, that is just the down payment". I think to myself, then why don't I. Dr. Sterner was terribly upset and signed me out "against medical advice".

After the wonderful experience post-delivery, the following day, Lou's sister and family of 2 young children arrived from Cleveland, Ohio for her husband's new assignment with the Boeing Company. What a wild time with 6 children under 4 years old. Steve and I went back to work at the store as the easy way out.

Ric is curious about the new baby. He says, "Steve was in your tummy huh?". I answer "yes". Ric thinks about that for a little while and then asks, "Is it all broke?" "No, it is not", I answer. "OK, then let me see", says Ric. I lift my shirt and show him that my tummy is still intact. He is really puzzled now about how Steve could get out without busting the tummy. I pass on education at the moment, later perhaps.

What a summer this has been. There have been six million visitors to the World's Fair here in Seattle, and I swear that half of them have been to our house. Eric's birthday was in July, so they bring birthday gifts for Eric and the tape arrived from the folks in Cleveland singing Happy birthday to Eric. Kris assumes that any gifts around here are for Eric, so she picks only the best flowers from the neighbor's yards and brings them home for Eric. Ric is still curious about the new baby and where it came from. He pets my tummy and asks the other day, "You got any more "bruzzers" in there?" I answer, "I certainly hope not." Ric says, "me too, I can't sleep with that baby crying all the time".

The cleaning business is taking up a great deal of time, both mine and Lou's. If one or the other is not down there, we are doing something related to the operations. Guess the kids have been watching too much television. They call Steve TV. When Marilyn took the kids to the supermarket there was a swinging door into the back room. Their comment was "Oh, there is the shooting show in there." When I do the laundry, they ask me if I am using the half clean laundry soap. One day Ric was on the floor doing exercises saying "No I don't, no I don't." When I asked what he was doing he says that Jack LaLanne said he would feel better if he did exercises. Steve has developed a strong grip once he gets hold of something. Ric says that he is going to "beteck" Steve, but he is not going to "beteck" those girls. I said that he should protect Kris and Lori and his mother just like his father does. Ric eats for about a half an hour in silence, and then says, "I can't "beteck" everybody." I was touched by his sincerity and concern and went over to kiss him. Lori pipes up, "miss me too, Mom".

Mom Clements sent us $20.00 for Christmas for the kids, so we bought a few things. Hope it is true that kids are happy with the little things. We have just a few days left in the business. We plan to put in a pressing machine and shoot the wad. If that does not work, we are bankrupt.

Life goes on in this house. When Lou started to sneeze the other day, he turned his head to the left, and there was Kris, so he turned his head to the right, and there was Eric, so he sneezed and hit Lori who got it at close range. Lou just shrugged his shoulders and wiped her up. Steve let out a yell one day when Kris was around him. I asked Ric to see what had happened as Kris is not very gentle. Ric came back all excited saying that Kris had knocked all his teeth out. Guess it was the first time that Ric realized that Steve did not have teeth yet. Life goes on.

$\mathcal{S}$even

A Fuller House

The Boeing Company is laying off employees by the gross and home builders are going bankrupt. One bankrupt builder was in the middle of making over an old farm house. It had missing lighting and plumbing fixtures, no closet doors or door knobs, but it had 5 acres with several outbuildings full of building materials. It is 2,800 sq. ft on the first floor with a half basement, 4 fireplaces, and a kitchen that is half the house. A big plus is a functional 20X 40 ft. swimming pool. We put a bid on it for half the asking price, and it was accepted.

Shortly after we moved in, my brother Dick was having a very hard time after a messy divorce and he had custody of his 3 girls. I offered to take them for the summer. The girls were all tied up inside after the mayhem at their house, cried a lot, wet the bed, and would fight at the drop of the hat. I hired a teen aged neighbor named Dawn to be a camp counselor and opened up one of the outbuildings as a hobby shop, got some art material, and have given Dawn my old camp and games book. The girls are relaxing a bit. We have a routine of crafts and nature trail hikes in the morning. This gives me time to clean, shop, prepare meals etc. We swim from 2:00 to 4:00 in the afternoon and have story hour after dinner from 7:00-8:00 PM. I take the crib full of cleaned clothes to fold while I watch as lifeguard. At 2:00 it looks like the pied piper has come through the neighborhood with a line of young people in their bathing suits with towels slung over their shoulders. They all came back for story time at 7:00 PM. We finished a great book called "The Box Car Kids". The girls related to that, as it was a story about 3 children who take care of themselves when they are left alone. The library is a wonderful place to go during the day to look for other books. We took trips to the countryside looking for just the right horse to buy. We have a barn to house it and pastures to roam. With 7 kids and usually Dawn and her brother Dwight, people usually looked at me like I am deranged which helps when trying to buy a horse. I got a series of 4 shots for the horse, a bridle and halter, a saddle, and free delivery. As I shook hands with the owner, he says, "Lordy woman, you should have been a horse trader, you are worse than most people I do business with".

Dick's girls are still a handful. I have chores for all according to their abilities. Nancy and Janice are good workers, but Gay tells me that she doesn't have to do anything. I say, "you are absolutely right, you don't have to ride the horse, you don't have to go with Dawn on nature hikes or make beautiful things in the hobby shop, you don't have to swim, or you don't even have to eat. I couldn't agree with you more. Let me know when you want to do something".

I had the kids take turns riding the horse around a ring with me holding the rope. I let each child take the horse on the road around the sheds. Janice came back without the horse and she was holding her arm crying. We took her to the doctor and he put her in a cast for her fractured radius. We returned to walking in a circle with a rope. This sweet looking Welsh pony turned out to be a rogue animal in that he would look for low tree limbs and gallop toward them to make sure nothing was left on his back on the other side. He would suddenly gallop and then make fast turns that usually set centrifugal force in motion sending the rider off in the original direction. I put a for sale ad in the newspaper. A doctor and his family bought it. When I found out he was a local physician, I said, "Oh good, you get free fracture service". I then wished I had a better language filter, but they bought the horse anyway.

We had a big pot of oatmeal with toast and jelly, went over to a friend's house to pick cherries, rode the horse, swam, and made a steak for dinner. We built a fire in the fireplace and roasted marshmallows, and when I asked the kids to go to bed, Gay says to her sisters that Aunt Lois is a witch. I found out what her trouble was. In Michigan, it gets dark at 7:00 PM. Washington latitudes do not get dark until about 10:00 PM. I read part of a letter to her father where she wrote "Aunt Lois puts us to bed in the daylight". It is hard to please some.

I loaded all 7 kids and Dwight into our old Volkswagen and went out to pick cucumbers to make pickles. We drove up to a vegetable stand in the valley and started pricing small cucumbers. The lady tending the stand says to her husband, "Look at that lady with all them kids, Charlie, get a bag." She proceeded to fill a big bag full of cucumbers for me and another bag of apples for the kids and wouldn't take any money. I insisted, but she refused. I didn't think too much about it until we visited the second stand. The lady gave Gay a bagful of ripe peaches to hand out to the kids. I have no idea where the bananas came from.

Eight

Trials and Tribulations

Lou's father had been dealing with cancer of the bowel and got the added diagnosis that it had spread to his brain. It was not long after this that his mother was alone and adrift. She moved into his sister's house where they built an addition room for her. Lou was so busy at the Boeing Company plus the dry cleaners that house chores were a bit behind. The basement had settlement cracks throughout and took on water. Lou said that it was not bad. Dawn's mother came over for coffee for the first time in the two years we lived there. The kids were playing down in the basement and came up stark naked and all wet. They asked for towels and their boat and said how much fun it was in that swimming pool. I explained to Fran that we had a little leak in our basement and went on talking. When Lou came home, I told him about the incident when we heard Steve from the other room saying, "I am going to grab that bad guy and take him down to the basement and throw him in the water". I smiled in my cup. Lou put his fork down and said, "OK, so I'll fix it".

Kid are different these days. We used to go outside and build snowmen. We got up late one Sunday morning, the kids were building a snowman alright, they had brought the snow inside the house and were building one in front of the fireplace and the television set.

Here it is June and we all have to get wormed again. The beds are stripped, sanitizing procedures to everything in sight, and the blankets dry-cleaned. I spent the morning wiping down walls, bedframes, and was at the cleaners with all the kids. I looked outside the store and saw the kids scraping wads of gum off the sidewalk and stuffing in their mouths as quick as they got a wad big enough to that which they were chewing. I had the feeling I was not using my time constructively.

One day I was in Lou's study looking out this second story window and saw my baby on the top of a tree limb flying past my window. I watched in horror as he safely climbed down the tree. I then saw a larger Eric climb up the flexible sapling that bent with his weight and rode it to the ground level. Then I heard him say, "fire two". I saw my other baby fly past the second story window. Lori squealed with delight and climbed down. They seemed to be having a good time, so I let them.

Lou and I were telling the kids that they were going to have another brother or sister. Ric said, "Oh no, the last one you had was a fink". Kris was disgusted and said, "Oh Mom, you won't even let me smoke". Lori said, "I can hardly wait to love him". Steve said, "Oh good, now I will be bigger than someone".

Beth arrive in this world Feb 4th, 1969. I was amazed to see her follow Lou's hand with her eyes at one day old. She could hold her head up immediately when placed on her tummy. At 6 weeks, she was turning over from tummy to back. Most amazing of all, she pushes up on her feet and can hold her own weight. She smiled from day one and makes communicating sounds. Aside from all of these startling things, she is beautiful (and this from a mother of 5). Lou as usual was present in the delivery room, and then stopped by the church on his way home to give a special prayer of thanksgiving for another healthy child and a safe delivery. We checked out of the hospital (against medical advice) and into the Hyatt House. It was a wonderful rest and the food so much better. The next day the family came down and we all had dinner in the room, watched television, and everybody got to love the new baby. One child got to stay overnight. The kids all left saying, "having babies is great Mom".

I never enjoyed a child as much as I did this one. With Ric, the first, I was afraid I would do something wrong. The rest came so fast that I ran nonstop just to maintain them. Each new addition was depleting and the pace exhausting without renewal. With this one, I am confident she is in good hands and I have enough quarters to feed the coin operated washing machine.

Aunt Ann (Sister Mary Famula) is my father's sister who spent her life as a Maryknoll Nun, primarily in Asia. She was Mother Superior for the school in Happy Valley, Hong Kong and a prisoner of the Japanese during the occupation in World War 2. She was returning home to the mother house in New York to retire. When passing through Seattle, she stopped to visit us in Seattle. I think she told a big fib about losing her passport and airline tickets because she wanted to spend time with our family. We set her up in the back room with her own bath and spent a lot of time making special recipes and hiking around the property. We took her on the ferry ride to Vashon Island and spent a few days camping out and exploring the beach and hiking around the island.

We also went to a horse auction one Sunday. She had been raised on a farm in Kentucky, where they raised horses and she loved them. We put all the kids in the car and took off. When we got there, she wanted to be inconspicuous in her black robes and white collar surrounding her face, so we moved up to the top row in the corner. We settled in and I took off Beth's clothes down to her diapers as it was a hot day, especially up that high. The kids went down to look over the horses for sale and came back all excited about one Welsh pony that was pure black. Beth had fallen asleep in my arms, so I handed her to Aunt Ann and went down to check out this pony. Beth woke up right after we left and saw the strange face in the black habit with the white collar around her face and began to scream. Here was Aunt Ann trying her best to be inconspicuous sitting alone in the corner of the top row at a horse auction with a screaming naked baby on her lap. She was furious with me and totally embarrassed. When we returned, she said with gritted teeth, "Don't you EVER do that to me again".

We bought the horse that the kids had fallen in love with during the auction and they wanted to go down and visit with her. Not wanting to leave Aunt Ann with the baby, we all went down to the paddock. The horses being auctioned were understandably excited and were kicking about in their stalls. Two huge stallions broke loose and began to run up and down the isles looking for an escape route. I pushed Aunt Ann and all the kids into an empty stall that was rich with manure up to our ankles and wait for someone to capture the two wild horses. No one stepped forward. I said out loud, "well, I guess the only way out of here is over that 8-foot fence." When I looked around, Aunt Ann was on top of the 8-foot fence and she hollered down to me, "hand me the baby." No sooner do I hand Beth over to her when Beth again feels threatened and begins to scream. It is really hard to look inconspicuous, dressed in a flowing black robe on top of an 8-ft fence holding a screaming naked baby. It was quiet on the way home. When I asked her how she was going to explain the hunks of horse manure all over her shoes and habit, she answered that she was going to tell them that I was not a good housekeeper. She does not even know about the worms yet.

In July of that year, what I thought was menopause, was really Joseph John on the way. Checking in, I told the doctor that I thought I was going to die. He informed me that he had some good news and some bad news. He added that I was going to live, but that I was pregnant.

Joey was a "10" without a mark. At 2 hours old, he could lift his head and look around. He follows sound and hand movements well, and he really woke up when he got circumcised. I really think it is cruel to have no anesthetic for these boys, for I am positive that Joe could feel the pain.

The puppies used to follow Beth as she crawled around the house, hoping she would throw up more milk. Now they can start all over again. The older kids will probably write notes on his hands like they did Beth, then send him into our room with one hand saying, "can we have", and on the other hand saying, "some pop". It is said that older mothers have higher birth rates of challenged children, and also higher birth rates of brilliant children. I honestly believe that I got the later, for both children are advanced in their motor skills. I was 42 years old in July of that year.

When Beth was about 8 years old, she came up to me one day and said, "I am glad I get to live in your house". I answered, "That is an unusual way to put it". Beth says, "I know". I said, "you just barely made it didn't you". Beth again answered, "I know". I looked at her beautiful face and said, "OK if you are so smart what is love?". Without hesitation, she said, "love is when you see someone with your heart". I looked at her a long time and said, "I have been trying to figure that one out for 40 years". Beth said without hesitation, "I know". I pulled my chair up next to her and said, "who are you anyway". Beth answered, "I am God's helper and my name is Beth." I pulled my chair up closer and asked, "why are you here?" Without hesitation Beth answered, "I am going to be a doctor and write books." "Where did you come from?" I asked. Beth replied while pointing up to the sky, "out there." I ask, "what is it like out there?" Beth answers, "It is cold and dark and full of short people". I laugh and say, "I wish I were smart enough to ask you more questions." Beth answers, "I know."

Two months later Lou got laid off from the Boeing Company. Boeing reduced their work force from 100,000 to what will be 20,000 employees. Unless you leave Seattle, there are no jobs. Even if you leave Seattle, there is very little in the aerospace area of Lou's expertise. He sent out 200 resumes and did not get one answer. He spent a lot of time in his office with the door closed.

In the course of a few days, things went from bad to worse. We were sued and spent 6 days in court. While gone, the front door at the Hub cleaners fell off of its hinges and broke into pieces. A pipe broke at the Lake Hills Cleaner, and we had to replace a 10-yard line of 6-inch cement. An insurance company called regarding a 5 car pile up on the freeway the day our horse broke out. The Arizona Land Company holding the paper on the acreage we thought we were purchasing went bankrupt, and the Internal Revenue sent us a letter informing us that we had been selected for audit.

In his early 40's, Lou is changing careers. A complete flip from research and development in aerospace engineering to a dry-cleaning plant owner and operator. In place of learning about how deep the dust is on the moon, he is now getting rid of dirt on this earth. Lesser men would crack under the stress of 6 babies to fed and engineers knee deep in unemployment lines. I remarked to Lou that Steve was wetting the bed and suggested that perhaps his life was not satisfying enough. Lou said that if that were any criteria, then I should have to be changing his sheets more often.

Nine

New Directions

Two years have passed since last entry. These have been grey days including financial disaster with accompanying self-doubt. We have added male and female menopausal symptoms and a house full of emerging teenagers. During these two years, we have closed the Hub Cleaners and the Lake Hills store was repossessed by the previous owner. The Newport Hills store was closed because the landlord would not renew the lease following a successful lawsuit by an existing dry cleaner with an exclusive lease clause. We sold all of our equipment for used parts, which netted us less than what was owed on the installation. Lou looked for a job in the aerospace field for months and I went back to work as a physical therapist for Group Health in Seattle. I remember leaving the house full of kids, driving down the road with abandon thinking, "is this a great country or what, and I SHOULD be doing this."

Group Health has outpatient clinics around the county. One doctor is writing a procedures manual for these clinics and I am writing the physical therapy portion for his book. I spent a lot of time in the library researching and loved the work. They were also opening a new clinic in Federal Way, a few blocks from our home. I hoped to be assigned to this clinic which would save several hours of driving. I had also been asked to apply as Temporary interim director for the new physical therapy school at the University of Puget Sound. They were looking for a PH. D as director, but I may get a crack at teaching. The family is now covered by health insurance. This has been bothering me for several years now, having 6 kids and no health insurance. Thank God we are all healthy.

The Watson clinic in Burien was where I had worked through the years on a part time basis. Grace Watson was getting ready to retire and called one day to ask if I would be interested in buying her out. She made an attractive offer of nothing down and the remainder to be paid on a monthly basis until the $200,000 was paid off. Lou and I talked and decided it was a positive move.

When I was applying to certify as a business, to bill insurance companies, the lady from Olympia named Marie showed up and we began the process. The Congress of the United States had just passed the new Medicare law. I was one of the few female private practice owners in the State of Washington. Marie was concerned about male practioners taking advantage of the new system and she liked me. She talked about the status of being a Rehabilitation Agency to me. I did not have a clue what a Rehabilitation Agency was, but if Marie wanted me to be an Agency, then I was going to be an Agency, whatever that was.

I was required to write a procedure manual and prepare my office to reflect all the new rules under which I was to operate. She shepherded me through the process and had me rewrite that which was needed and lacking. I finally got the certification as a Rehabilitation Agency. What I did not know was that this status now allowed me to bill Medicare direct. One day there was a few hours that I was not scheduled. I walked to the nursing home down the block in Burien, looked for the superintendent's office and suggested that I could treat their patients for rehabilitation. He bought the idea and I found myself suggesting to the attending physicians what I could do for their patients to improve the quality of their lives and possibly have them return to independent living. In a private practice, you hire therapists on salary. There are many days when you are paying your staff for the day, but the schedule will include many hours without a scheduled patient. This was a way to fund this unscheduled time for a private practice.

This was working out well for our clinic. One day I went to another more distant nursing home to see what was possible. I saw a lady coming down the hall and I liked her. I stopped and asked her for directions. We got to talking and she asked me to sit down and have some coffee with her. I explained how as a Rehabilitation Agency, I could come in and treat patients, improving the quality of care at no cost to them, as I could bill Medicare direct. She took me by the hand and we walked into the superintendent's office. She explained my mission in terms he understood. I walked out of there with a contract for 7 nursing homes. They were a chain of nursing homes around the State.

It occurred to me that now I had a problem, as therapists were scarce and difficult to hire. There was a state-wide physical therapy private practice section meeting to be held in the near future that I attended. I was the only woman there. I stood up and said that I could fund their down time. I explained that if they got the nursing homes in their cities to agree to sign a contract with me, that I could pay their therapists on their down time at double their salaries while in their local nursing homes treating patients.

The therapists said if you can do this, why can't we? I informed them that as an Agency, you are paid an INTERIM REIMBURSEMENT for an entire year on your ALLOWABLE costs. At the end of the year, you submit a cost report and based on their ALLOWABLE COSTS, you either owe them more money, or they pay you more. More likely than not, you will owe them a lot of money. For example, whatever salary you are now paying yourself, Medicare may decide a big chunk of that is not ALLOWABLE. Same with equipment purchases, continuing education, company promotions, vacations, etc. Essentially you sell your independence. If you want to do this, I will show you how for $2,000. If you work for me for a year, I will show you how for nothing. I spent the next several months going around the state signing up nursing homes (for a contract fee of $300) and ended up having 60% of the nursing homes in the State of Washington under contract. I had no idea what was possible and no precedent to emulate, but I felt guided and empowered like no other time in my life.

Medicare did experience some fraud and abuse and began to tighten the screws on honest practioners along with those undeserving. Over time, with too many bad experiences and unreasonable denials, it became desirable to decertify. For example, the same people doing the same procedure had claims suddenly 100% denied because the Medicare staff had been to a meeting and they changed all the rules without telling us what they had done and why they had done this. Many practioners had paid their staff as usual and now had to mortgage their homes or borrow money in order to stay in business. It took many troubled years to straighten everything out, but I preferred to return to private practice where the gross was not as large, but the net was predictable and so much less stressful, and in the end just as rewarding financially.

I was able to buy a building near the hospital that was a perfect location for a budding practice. Unfettered, the business provided many perks like continuing education trips that were tax deductible, my automobile was a business expense, health insurance and pension plan contributions for the staff expanded.

Learning a lot about how to maneuver taxes and accounting was empowering and exciting. I loved the growth, the pleasure and excitement, the opportunities available secondary to being in business, and the knowledge that anything was possible.

Lou began a consulting business that he could run out of the home that was successful. His being home while the kids were still in the nest gave me the opportunity to spread my wings and fly. What a wonderful ride.

As the Rehabilitation Agency business was a new entity, at one of the National Physical Therapy Associations meeting, we formed a new Organization called the National Association of Rehabilitation Agencies (NARA). I became the first national secretary that required more travel (that was an allowable cost). I spent one month in China with a medical team that got access to communes and even the Beijing Hospital. We witnessed a gall bladder surgery with an acupuncture anesthetic. I asked the physician when do they usually use acupuncture for an anesthetic. He answered, "When there are tours". I asked if it was good, why would they just use it when there are tours. His answer was that it took several hours to get the patient prepared for surgery but with a needle, it took only minutes. I could write a book about China in 1988.

I went to an international conference in France and sailed the French Riviera on the way home. Beth was finishing her last semester of college in Italy and called to say that she was not coming home. I asked why, and she said that she was going to tour. I mentioned that she didn't have any money to do that. She told me that she would think of something. My first thought was that she was going to sell her body. That is when I decided to invite her to sail the French Riviera, so we would have some quality time to talk. I asked some of my beginning sailing class to form a team. We all met in Paris in time for the Tour De France and took the train down to Toulon. One of the ladies owned two health food stores and was a great sales person. By the end of two weeks, Beth was convinced that she wanted to be a naturopathic physician and spent the next 4 years completing that training.

We spent many happy years sailing. I taught with the Tacoma Women's

Sailing Association for 20 years each spring and fall. We would gather after work at 6:00, sail until dark, party until midnight, and most slept on the boat and returned to work refreshed the following morning. What a wonderful way to meet new friends. There were usually 8 -10 boats going out. One of the best parts was that the teachers would go somewhere in the world to sail for 2 weeks each year. We sailed many Greek Islands. One year we sailed the path of Ulysses coming home from the Trojan wars. We sailed the Australian Whitsunday Islands, New Zealand, the Italian coast, The French Riviera, Tahiti, Tonga, Figi, the inside passage toward Alaska, The Greater and Lesser Antilles, Virgin Islands, Granada, many Gulf Islands and so many San Juan Island excursions.

Lou and I would sail each year a couple of trips up to the San Juan and Gulf Islands and, of course, many local jaunts like over to Tacoma for dinner or over to Gig Harbor on New Year's Eve for their midnight marathon and party. We always wanted a sailboat in front of the house, so we built our dream house at Pleasant Harbor that had a 4,000 ft interior and was large enough to sleep the family of 30 if we used the motor home and the boat for quarters. We lived across from F dock at the Pleasant Harbor Marina and had the use of the hot tub and the 60 ft. swimming pool, plus the restaurant and reading-media room. We could dingy over, swim or walk over to use all the facilities.

Lou had his office on the lower floor which had its own kitchen, 3 baths, a beautiful view of the Harbor with a 150 ft. deck. His consulting business flourished. As an engineer, he got into a nitch business of Quality Consulting. When a large construction firm was hired to do a job over a certain dollar figure, the contract requirements included that an outside inspector be hired to insure the required structures were built according to plan. Lou provided this service and had a list of qualified inspectors he hired to do these jobs. On occasion we would take the motor home and inspect these jobs and as the years went by, he not only went nationwide, but international on some overseas jobs as well. He continued to run Quality Consultants well into his 80's, and his office is as he left it as we speak in our Florida home.

Ten

The Villages

The Villages have over 100 miles of golf cart trails and you can get to anything on your golf cart. I have seen motorized wheelchairs on the golf cart trails going to anything you can get to in a car within the Villages, keeping people functioning independently well beyond their driving years. There are multiple support services that allow this continuing quality of life for so many years beyond the norm. There are 3,500 clubs. If you have an interest, there is a club. There are superior medical facilities, meal services, cleaning and landscaping, but most of all a community of people who have worked hard all their lives, have been successful, are proud of what they have accomplished, and willing to share their blessings with others. I absolutely love our neighbors and this community who are focused on fitness and fun with a purpose driven life. Most are into some sort of outreach activity like the food kitchen in the surrounding towns, or tutoring at the local school districts, volunteering at the local hospital or health facilities. Churches are well attended. Our church for example has a filler factory where they meet from 8:00 AM to noon 2 days a week to make things to put in shoe boxes that go out at Christmas for the Franklin Graham Samaritan's Purse Foundation. The first year they made 600 boxes, the next they put together 2,000 boxes, and the following year it was 11,000. This year we put together 14,400 boxes. What started out as a fruitful activity turned into a magnet for new church members. The members telling their neighbors about how excited they were about what they were doing with their time, incentivized them to join the filler factory because they wanted something significant in their lives.

There are 65 golf courses here in the Villages and 65 recreation centers, each with a different theme. Our neighborhood ladies play once or twice a week and then go out to lunch. There are couples' groups doing the same. There are 3 Village Squares, each with live music every night from 5:00 to 9:00. (not much happens after 9:00). The list goes on. Village people have been tested with other communities of the same age and found that this higher quality of active life gives the average person an added 10 "good" years to that of the average norm.

I believe that these last years were the best of our lives. We went to swim aerobics regularly 3X per week. It is heavy exercises in the water taught by an 85-year-old woman who talks about going zip lining. We had Fridays as our date night where we went to the Philosophy Club with always thought-provoking topics, and then out to dinner. We loved the activities in our dynamic church with the outdoor movies and concerts on the screen with a stage built onto the side of the church that you can attend in your golf carts or bring a pizza and chairs. Lou would get up in the morning and read the newspaper on the screened in the lanai by the pool with a hot cup of coffee before heading off to his office to look for new contracts and someone to fill them. I had dinner on the table at 6:00 PM every night, with attention to his favorite cheese, homemade bread, and a great selection of Italian olives and condiments.

Five years ago, we went to his yearly physical exam. We were both very healthy into our 80's. His doctor said there was some concern with his blood test and sent us to a specialist who would check it out. What a surprise it was when we walked into the clinic assigned with the name "Lake Sumpter Cancer Institute". Surely, we must be in the wrong place. The diagnosis was Chronic Lymphocytic Leukemia. For the next 4 years, we were handling this diagnosis. We were very careful with the diet, infection control, exercise, and rest. Our daughter Beth was then a practicing Naturopathic Physician, gave us the proper supplements and instructions in and use of the BEMER. The BEMER is an adjunct to the circulatory stimulation. By lying on this body pad that has within it a 10 HZ pulse followed by a 30HZ pulse and is set up for an 8-minute treatment 2X per day. All it does is stimulate the circulatory system to increase the blood flow to the sluggish capillaries that become smaller and smaller as they enter the end organs. As we age, the circulatory system becomes more sluggish. Fewer and fewer blood corpuscle enter the end organs, diminishing their function until the systems do not support one another. The quality of life diminishes followed by death.

We rechecked with the doctor every 4 months and were pleased to find that Lou was "holding" in his blood counts, not taking the normal deteriorating course of blood count tests with this diagnosis. The doctor each time just said it varied and made another appointment. On one appointment I told the doctor that I had a confession to make. He was mildly interested. I went on to say that we had a daughter who was a naturopathic physician. He threw his eyes back and then refocused. I went on to tell him that she had Lou on a list of supplements that she had prescribed for him, and then went on to tell him about the Bemer that we used every day. His response was that if it made her happy, to keep on doing that.

As we walked out of the office, I noticed a room full of people with iv's up their arms and bags of medicines at their sides. I wondered about radiation opportunities and where that might be and thought about how many of them would benefit from what Lou was doing if they did not have such a pompous physician.

Lou was not at the stage of his blood work that he was on the "normal path" of treatment, but he was sleeping more often and longer during these naps. I knew the path and prayed more often.

It was our Friday date night and we went to the Philosophy Club and out to dinner. At dinner, we exchanged on a deeper level than I remember, giving thanks for being so healthy, living in these Villages, living this life where anything was possible and limited only by our imaginations and energy. We discussed how pleased we were with our children leading mostly productive lives with problems controlled. How nice to have a family that loves and enjoys one another. We discussed how they enjoyed each other so much that they sometimes forgot to invite us. The next morning, Lou got out of bed to put his bathing suit to go to swim aerobics, then fell naked out of the closet on to the floor in the hallway with strange gurgling sounds. I raced up to him and he raised his hand and tried to talk but could not make any sounds. I called 911. I heard the siren in a very few moments and 3 wonderful men came in and took over. They flew him to the Orlando Regional Medical Center because they deemed he needed to be there in a hurry. They suspected a brain bleed. They were so professional and effective, we are truly blessed here in these Villages with the services available.

This was the last time I saw Lou moving.

Eleven

The Personal Reconstruction

As I watched the emergency team load my husband into the ambulance, I called Patrick, a good friend. I asked him if he would go with me to the Orlando Hospital as Lou was in the ambulance with a probable stroke. He agreed to be right over. When I finished that call, I made another one to Jeremy, to tell him not to come that evening, as something had come up. He was scheduled to come to our house with his wife and two children in their motor home for a week or two.

The entire following week was the most life changing chain of events that I have ever experienced. When we got to the hospital in Orlando, the doctor told me that Lou had had a catastrophic brain injury and if left unsupported, he would probably not last the day. It was my call to apply life support. The doctor said he would not suggest it, as Lou would always need to be tube fed, be totally dependent, and would probably never leave a nursing home. At that moment, I could only try to save his life, and requested life support. I was certain that no matter how debilitated he was, that I could help him rehabilitate and lead a life worth living. I was a physical therapist and knew what needed to be done to make this happen. Once life support is applied, to remove it is a legal problem.

The sequence of events that followed was a spiritual awareness of HIS presence that was so evident, that I began to feel a deep gratitude for this blessing. I listened for and responded to HIS guidance. The following is segmented into specific illustrations of this presence.

JEREMY

We were building a house on the waterfront at Pleasant Harbor, Washington and Jeremy was a teenage handyman working on our project. I had just retired and found it fun that first year to drive one hour and a half from Seattle to Brinnon and spend two days painting all the cedar siding with 3 coats of cetal stain, inside and out, before it was installed. I would spend one night on my sailboat moored in the harbor. I got to know the crew well that year. When I asked why I had to paint the inside of the boards, the contractor said that moisture collects behind the boards, pushes forward and deteriorates the exterior finish over time. I saw the wisdom of this procedure ten years later when the house exterior looked like it had just been painted. The master carpenter said he could always tell when the owner painted because he never got splinters when he installed the siding. When Jeremy graduated from high school, he went to Moody Bible College and got his degree. Lou and I contributed to his tuition along with our church body. He became a helicopter pilot with the New Tribes Mission and delivers supplies, equipment and personnel to remote tribal areas in underdeveloped areas of the world. These missionaries are required to generate enough financial funding to support their mission. Jeremy was spending 6 months in the United States generating financial sources to continue his work when he called us and requested permission to visit us with his motor home and family for a short while. We agreed to host them.

He was scheduled to arrive on Saturday, the day that my husband Lou had his massive bleed. When I saw Lou crawl out of the closet, roll over on his back and stare into space while trying to speak, I knew he needed help. I called 911 and the ambulance was there in minutes. While they were preparing to transport him to the hospital, I called Jeremy and told him not to come as something had come up. With the phone in my hand, the ambulance driver came up to the door and said, "change of plans, we are going to helicopter him to the Orlando Regional Medical Center, he has a bleed and we need to get him there in a hurry". I simply said into the phone, "I have to go now" and hung up.

Patrick drove with me for the hour and a half trip to Orlando. We arrived at the emergency room just after diagnostic procedures had been completed. The doctor said that he had a massive cerebral vascular accident and would probably not live through the day. I called my son Steve and said that I wanted him to talk to his father's doctor and handed him the phone. The neurosurgeon introduced himself and explained that his father had a massive embolism in his brain and it was inoperable. He would continue to bleed and would not last much longer. He recommended that if he wanted to see his father before he passed than he make immediate plans to come. Steve took emergency leave and the first flight out the following morning.

We accompanied Lou to the adjoining Hospice unit and were seated in the waiting room when who should show up but Jeremy. I could not figure out how in the world he would know to come here at this time. Jeremy had heard the ambulance driver tell me they were going to fly him to the Orlando Regional Medical Center while I was on the phone with him. He got a newspaper and looked up local churches. The first church he called to ask their recommendation for where he could park his motor home and family for few days while he took care of his mission business and why the sudden change of plans. The pastor told him that they had just this week finished a plot next to their church, with all the hook ups for one motor home, and that he would be welcome to be the first to stay. He was sure that God had just sent him his first guest.

Jeremy parked the motor home and left his family at the church plot. He detached his small car for the drive to Orlando. It was a Saturday and the traffic mercifully low for Orlando. He arrived shortly after we did with a bag full of fruit, cheese and crackers, some bottled water, and fruit juices with some M&M candies. Jeremy and Patrick stayed with us through the afternoon. Pastor Bob and his wife Vicky from our Live Oaks Church arrived later that day. Patrick had called the church and notified them of Lou's condition.

My first awareness of HIS presence was when Pastor Bob put his arm around me in front of Lou's body and prayed with me. I felt a warmth beginning in my abdomen and rise up through my chest, my throat, then my head, and felt an immediate calm that was lasting. I felt blessed and appreciated. Pastor Bob offered Patrick a ride back to the Villages.

I thanked Jeremy for coming and made it known that I would really like to be alone with Lou in the hospice room that had a sleeping couch for me. The hospice staff have to be very special people. They were specialists in making life as it is the best possible for families. I will always be grateful to every one of these special people.

About 6:00 PM my cell phone rang. It was Jeremy. He said, "would you like to have dinner with me?" I asked, "where are you?" He said," in the waiting room, I thought you would like some company and I wanted to make sure you had something to eat besides cheese and crackers."

We went down to the cafeteria and selected mostly salads. Jeremy told me about his recent mission to Papua New Guinea. He now has two young children and a supportive wife who is thriving under the lifestyle of a minimalist with a purpose driven life. Jeremy loves to talk excitedly about his work. It was almost midnight when I told him I really needed to try to sleep. I told him that my son Steve was arriving the following morning at 7:00 AM from Seattle, and I thanked him for his loving attention that was so much appreciated.

Jeremy drove the hour and a half back to the Villages and then got up at 5:00 AM to meet Steve at the airport to bring him directly to the hospital and then spent the rest of the day with us.

Our son Steve is very adept at communications. He arranged the heartwarming Veteran's ceremony and made arrangements for all the other siblings to be on a conference call to participate in the ceremony and say their own good byes to their father. Steve also presented them with the brain scan that showed the massive brain bleed and requested the removal of the life support which the doctor initiated shortly afterward. It was only a matter of hours from that point for the final breath to quietly leave his body.

Pastor Lee from our Live Oaks Church made the trip to the hospital and was present for the ceremony also. Jeremy, Lee, Steve and I were sitting in Lou's room talking. To introduce them to each other, I mentioned that Jeremy had just gotten back from Papua New Guinea as a helicopter pilot delivering supplies and personnel to remote areas. Pastor Lee told us about his latest assignment as Administrator of the Evangelical Seminary where one of his professors had just spent 10 years translating the bible from English into the new Guinea languages, of which there are many. I was astounded at the chain of events happening as I sat here beside Lou's still warm body. The week before I had gotten an e-mail from friends in Australia who were Christian loggers who operated a logging company. They were coming to America and asked if they could visit us while here. I had heard the story about one of their employees who was married to a woman from New Guinea who inherited 2 million acres of land, but because she was a woman, could not receive it. Her husband could. Being a simple logger, he did not know what to do with this, so he went to his bosses and spoke with them. The Christian employers pondered over this and decided that they could go to the New Guinea government and offer them 15% for permits and permission to selectively log this land, give 15% to the indigenous population they displaced, put 50% toward building churches, hospitals, schools, wells, power, infrastructure, residences, 10% for costs, and 10% for profit. They were into their 3rd year and I asked how the project was progressing. Christine wrote back that there had been tough years with destructive storms, wars, disease, earthquakes, etc. but that the project was moving forward. She added that when most NG tribes have conflicts, they kill each other, but the Christian tribes negotiate.

I thought sitting beside Lou's still warm body that this New Guinea connection was shouting out to me that we needed to connect the loggers with the bible translators and the helicopter pilot. We sat there and exchanged e-mails and phone numbers for all to connect for the common good. What a powerful moment to be a part of this work for God's glory.

In the meantime, back in Wildwood, Jeremy's wife and children were being introduced to the Sunday congregation. She shared their story and a video of the New Guinea mission. When Jeremy returned from Orlando, he wanted to thank the pastor for his hospitality. With his formative skills as a construction worker, he noted a contribution he could make to his motor home site, the church, and the parsonage. With the help of some of the parishioners he made some upgrades during the next few days. They were so grateful that this poor church raised $2,500 for his mission. I matched that contribution, and overall it was a good week for all.

Jeremy left me with a thumb drive with over an hour of videos of the tribal Christian growth and the people who are spending their lives teaching about the love of Jesus and the impact they are having in promoting good over evil in the remote areas. Our pastor believes that the church is not the building, but the place where people come to learn to make Jesus famous. We are a strong mixture of teachers, doctors, nurses, construction workers, plumbers, everything you need to build communities of hard working and God-fearing families with strong values and sustainable positive lives. HIS presence continues to be felt with a power that surpasses understanding. Does this connection have legs, I stand in awe.

STEVE

Steve placed the cell phone down and tapped the back several times with his index finger. The neural surgeon had just explained that his father was hours away from passing and that he had only a few hours if he wanted to see him alive. Minutes before he was getting ready for church and now, he felt as if someone had given him a kick in the solar plexus. He breathed a deep sigh as he looked at the ceiling for several minutes and then acted. His thought was that his mother could not go through this alone. He immediately made the earliest reservation to Orlando, Florida with a return ticket to Settle in one week.

He and Jeremy arrived at the hospital midafternoon the next day in time to see his father being moved from the emergency room to adjoining hospice facility. Steve saw the CAT scan, where the doctor pointed out all the outing white areas as the bleed areas that surrounded the skull casing, as well as the brain stem and their surrounding areas. The finality was obvious to him and he comforted his mother who was questioning her decision to put his father on life support. He explained this enabled him to get there in time for himself and the rest of the family to be there for his passing. His mission was to convince his mother that he had made the right decision to let nature take its course. What kind of a life would it be for his father to live as a total dependent devoid of any quality of life.

As we moved into the hospice facility and we sat in the waiting room as they prepared both Lou and his room, we talked about the past, the present, and what was about to take place. What began as another ordinary day morphed into a life changing event in the blink of an eye. His parents had been married for 62 years, spawning 6 children and 20 grandchildren. Together they had hosted holidays, multiple family reunions, spontaneous get togethers, all of which was about to change. The veteran's ceremony, conference calls with siblings, and once the breathing tubes were removed, it was only a matter of hours for life to cease.

The following week Steve went into his father's office to get his papers in order to see what bills had to be paid, what accounts needed to be closed, what legal issues and notifications needed to be conducted etc. What was so difficult was that there are "no people" on the other end of a phone, just a recording directing you to push certain buttons or direct you to another waiting recording to proceed in what may or may not be what you wanted in the first place. A half an hour wait on the phone was the norm to get to another recording. Essentially a very frustrating week for Steve while dismissing his own grief to better address the grief of his mother.

It was the last day of his visit while we were on a mission to see a notary to finalize important papers that needed to be sent. Picture Steve driving the round-a-bouts while his mother was talking to a friend on the phone directing his movements. She was worried and aware of the unusual rules of the road for the uninitiated nonresident. With some irritation he told her that he knew how to drive. On the second round-about, Steve called his mother a "nagavator". On the third round-a-bout she was still telling him how to navigate while on the phone and a third admonition from him that he didn't require help to drive a car. He pulled over to the side of the road, turned off the car and said, "I have had it, I cannot do this anymore, I am through." He got out of the car, handed the keys to her, got in the passenger seat, and folded his arms with his eyes closed.

She was heart sick for she realized what she had done and how he must be feeling. She got into the driver's seat and silently drove the car toward the Notary office. She remembered a CD that Steve had made of his singing with a guitar that she kept in the car. She fumbled around, found it, placed it in the CD player, thinking this might make him feel better. A song came up, and it was beautiful. She looked over and Steve was wiping tears from his eyes. He said through the tears, "Those are the last words that I said to my father when I placed my hand on his still warm forehead just before it turned cold."

The words were, "and with your final heartbeat, kiss the world goodbye, go in peace and laugh on glory's side, and fly to Jesus, fly to Jesus and live".

She pulled over to the curb and thought, what are the chances that I would remember a CD that had been in the car for years without being touched, that I would put this CD in at that moment, and THAT song would come up first among a list of songs that were on this recording without some Devine intervention.

She took his hand and said, "This has to be God talking to you, telling you to forgive an old lady who is in pain."

We hugged for a long time contemplating the impact of this moment, and then drove on in silence. Angst was replaced by a peace that was now permeating the car, with a renewed appreciation of HIS unmistakable presence.

KISS THE WORLD GOODBYE

On his final breath the room began to empty, and I was left alone to deal with the reality of what had just happened. At first, I was just numb. I moved closer and put my hand on his forehead and expressed that I wished I had been a better wife and wished with all my heart that I had that opportunity. I seldom cry but found myself sobbing. Through the tears, I gathered my things and joined a line of mourners waiting outside the door ready to offer loving support for which I was grateful.

I was also grateful to the hospice staff. I vaguely remember Steve and I standing at their desk and them explaining my next steps following the notice of a death. Decisions needed to be made about choices of what, when, and where to reclaim Lou's remains. I vaguely remember choosing cremation. I knew that I wanted all my children to participate in his celebration of life and burial. Transporting his ashes to Washington was the answer.

This seamless transition felt like someone outside of myself was directing all events and I was just a bystander. I do not know if I could have made any decisions or contemplate what actions I should be taking without Steve by my side during my own personal fog at that point. It was like someone else oversaw all my moves. I couldn't even remember where I had parked my car in relation to where we were now located. I just remember how blessed I felt to have Steve taking care of all the details of checking out of the hospice and hospital and finding our way out of the traffic that is like a zoo in Orlando, and back to the now empty house at the Villages.

How strange it was to walk into the house knowing that life from this day forward would be different. I did not know at the time, that I was different, living a different life with a different focus. I felt God's presence and was so grateful for all of my blessings and knew the peace of being a Christian like never before in this lifetime.

I began the next day to focus on all the things I should be grateful for.

1. That Lou had left this world peacefully with all of his facilities at a happy time in his life, minus all the pain and suffering that a majority of people must endure.
2. That he left me with a wonderful functioning family and financial wherewithal to continue life as we had known it, free to pursue a purpose driven life unencumbered by debt or physical disabilities.
3. I was grateful for the incredible health I have always enjoyed and felt that surely God has a purpose for the use of this gift. I had been so aware of HIS presence these past days that I felt that God put me in this place at this time for the purpose of being used in HIS service. My job up to now has been to prepare a home and offer family service. From this day forward, my job is to look for work on HIS behalf and use my skills, good physical and financial health for a worthy purpose. Let me be worthy of being used in your service and let me be an instrument of your peace. I am HIS from this day forward.

YVONNE AND ALICE

On the day I came home from the Orlando Hospital where I left Lou's body for the Neptune Society to cremate, I came home to an empty house and the full impact that from this day forward, life would be different than it had been in the past 62 years. I looked across the street and saw a moving truck unloading furniture into the empty house. I found out that a recent widow was moving in and had arrived with her 2 daughters. They came to make sure that she would be safe and happy in her new life here in the Villages. It occurred to me that Lou would not be needing the ticket to the neighborhood monthly social event, so I went across the street, rang the doorbell and introduced myself. Her daughters were excited about my offering to take Yvonne to a local social event as a harbinger of good things to come for her. On the day of the event, I picked her up and we settled at a table that housed some friends of mine, introduced her to them, and proceeded to enjoy the evening. Among the table participants was another lady named Alice whose husband had died the month before Lou passed away. As always, at the end of the evening, they have a drawing of door prizes selected from all purchased tickets. The first prize went to Alice at our table. The next drawing went to Yvonne at our table who said she never wins prizes, and the third prize went to me, who was very surprised. We all received a unique bottle of Vodka that had lighted messages flashing on the insert that was changeable by pushing on a series of available selections like HAPPY BIRTHDAY, HAPPY NEW YEAR, MERRY CHRISTMAS, CONGRATULATIONS. Rarely do the prizes go to the same people at one table. It occurred to me that we are all recent widows and maybe God was sending his solace and warmth to the ones who needed it the most on this day. I prefer to give thanks to HIM rather than some lucky star. I was already beginning to feel the flow that comes when working in HIS service, and it felt good.

PRACTICING SENSIVITY

After Steve left for home, our daughter Kris came to spend the week with me. The siblings had gotten together to make sure that Mom had all the support she needed to make the new life transition. It was heartwarming to know that our children cared and planned. Kris provided a different kind of support than the business side of transition. She was into cleaning out the refrigerator and taking care of all house tasks and normal living duties. The kids had all signed up to spend their "week" with Mom for which I was touched and comforted. I did not find that complicating their lives was necessary. After 2 weeks of mind clearing, of being loved and nurtured, having just had the amazing experience of HIS presence for one full week during this life changing event, I felt ready to begin my new life of service. I said to Kris, "How can I get along with my life if you kids keep showing up?"

Kris thoroughly understands me and knew that it was time. I impressed upon her how much their love and caring meant to me, and how they all had allowed me to adjust to my new reality with the knowledge that I had a lot of support and could call on any of them at any time that I felt the need. I indeed have been blessed in this lifetime. I moved on with a full heart.

SENSITIVITY TRAINING

My first "job" came at the local mail delivery station where the neighborhoods go to pick up their mail. I saw a dear old friend walking up and she looked weary and sad. She has been taking care of a 35-year-old son that is mentally challenged. I am not usually aware of when people look sad or not, but uncharacteristically I said to her, "I do not see enough of you. If I invited you and John over to dinner, would you come?" She immediately said no. I asked her why not. Her answer was, "because John cannot swallow, he has been diagnosed with esophageal cancer, and he does not know it yet." I swallowed and teared up at the horrible news. I took her arm and said, "sorry, I am not used to "leaking" at the post office but know that I care."

I thought of what I could do and decided that the most helpful thing was to notify select people in this wonderful neighborhood that we have in this Florida bit of paradise that there was someone in our neighborhood that needed our love and why. I was pleased to see that during the Christmas Golf cart parade the lead car had in the front seat a smiling John, and the men in the neighborhood took John on their golf carts when they played golf, and at the monthly neighborhood Rec Center gathering, they had a tournament that divided the participants into teams with a dollar prize that netted the team $200 to split among them. In their Toga attire (which was the theme of the night) after the tournament was over, they all marched over in their costumes to John's house and presented John with their hard-earned prize money. John was delighted to be so honored. He and his Mom went to the store and purchased some video games that he had wanted and promptly put them to good use. I do not know if my efforts had any part on community support, but it felt good to think that it did.

I can't tell you of the joy that comes from spending your time looking for ways to bring joy and peace to other people. To always be looking for the opportunity to spread the "good news" about God's presence.

WHOLE NEW WAY TO LIVE

Lou's favorite toy was his motor home. When we went somewhere, I was always the support person and the substitute driver. When we sailed the boat, he was the line handler and tie up person. I loved living in the Florida Villages, but missed the kids who lived in Washington State. Lou loved his home and a sailboat was not in his planning. I always kidded Lou about, "when one of us goes, I am going to buy a sailboat to live on in the summer." One of my neighbors kept sending me e-mails from Yacht World magazine with tantalizing advertisements of boats for sale. We owned a moorage slip in Pleasant Harbor Washington. With 6 children there and me loving the Villages, it seemed plausible that to buy a sailboat to fill the slip that I was already paid for was a reasonable purchase. There would be no property taxes, there was 24 hr. surveillance, and I could visit the family without disturbing their lives. They could have a condo at the beach free to use all year long.

I found the biggest boat that I could put in my slip. It was a 38 ft. Beneteau sailboat with stellar credentials. On a leap of faith, I bought an airline ticket to Sidney British Columbia and put earnest money on it so that it would not be sold before I got there. The boat was perfect. It had been owned by a couple who obviously loved it, but had to give it up because the wife had contracted multiple sclerosis and it was no longer safe for her to be on it. The boat came with everything provided including dishes, linens, climbing gear, a full winter cover, and had just been bottom painted that year. One man offered me $10,000 to walk away. The subsequent survey proved the worth of the boat and the deal was that was to be delivered to my slip in Pleasant harbor. The deal was sealed.

MIKE AND DONNA

On the day the Beneteau was delivered to Pleasant Harbor, we met Mike and Donna June. Kris was with me on the day the sailboat was delivered. She saw a pleasant middle-aged man coming down the dock carrying some blow-up pool toys. She jokingly said to him, "did you have a good time at the pool?" He looked at them hastily and responded that they were for his grandchildren. Kris, wanting to make her point, says, "you don't expect me to believe, that do you?" They both laughed and Mike said, "Oh look at that beautiful Beneteau boat coming in. Kris said, "Oh that's my 'mom's boat". Mike said, "boy, would I love to sail that." Kris mentioned that her mom was at the pool and why not come up and introduce yourself. Long story short, Mike and Donna did come back to the pool and talk about his love of sailing and his experience. Mike had sailed for years but bought a motor boat for the safety of his two grand kids. He and Donna were devoted to making wonderful memories for these two girls.

This was a like a blessing from heaven to me, because at my age, I bought this boat to live on, but never expected to leave the dock. It became a further blessing when he said that he had just retired as a canvas boat cover manufacturer. This gem of a boat has a winter cover that I cannot even lift. When I asked if he would put on my winter cover, he immediately agreed to do this. I offered to pay him, and his answer was that he would rather get paid by sailing with me. Long story short, that very day, we were out sailing. We sailed several times which was a dream beyond my wildest expectations.

On one sailing trip, we talked about Lou's recent death, and I sent him a copy of a talk I gave at Lou's memorial just held at the Marina. In it, I discussed HIS unmistakable presence and how it energized me in place of depression and pity parties at my new status of being a widow, and a focus on finding jobs at being used in HIS service. Mike revealed that he and Donna had two daughters, one of which was killed in an automobile accident 10 years ago. Donna said that Mike turned his back on the church and anything to do with it since that time.

My sensors were alerted, and I knew my role going forward. Being new at this, I needed to do this right. I started by telling Mike about my journey from being a casual Christian to a believer when I met Rob VanDeWeghe, who just published a book called PREPARED TO ANSWER. He gave talks for any who wanted to listen prior to church in Quilcene on Sunday morning before the 10:00 service. Lou and I went each Sunday and argued with this wonderful patient man for nearly a year. When we got to "The Shroud of Turin", I did some research to be armed for the Sunday meeting, and found there was a conference of International scientists at the Ohio State University in March of 2010 with recorded sessions of the entire week. I spent the following week listening to these wonderful researchers and at the end of the which, I turned into a believer.

I mentioned this reference to Mike, who said he was a skeptic and wanted more than emotional idle chatter. Later I got an e-mail that said he had accessed the Google site and found that there was a Washington State International Shroud Conference in July of 2017, and this is what he learned from this one that was not in the March conference.

I grew to love Mike and Donna, and I knew that sailing a boat was so much better for the boat than to just sit in the nonmoving waters. This boat became "our boat". I left word at the marina office that Mike had my permission to take the boat out anytime he wanted. I gave him a set of keys and encouraged him to use them.

The first winter, Mike went to my boat often to run the engine to keep the valves lubricated and checked the winter cover to check for leaks. He would send me updates on the progress. I sent them a package of Omaha steaks like the rest of the family.

When I arrived the following June, the boat winter cover had been removed and was the cleanest looking boat on the dock. He helped me prepare the fresh water for purity, but the best part was that he agreed to take two sets of guests out for an overnight at Alderbrook, the ultra-resort, a day's sail down Hood Canal. I am planning a tandem trip for next year with Mike and Donna to the San Juan Islands with Eric and Ann, and a couple from our church who are sailors.

A recent e-mail from Mike makes me feel good about my mission. He says, I admit that I would love to have your faith and hope that someday I do. I can say that your friendship has been very special to Donna and me. There seems to be a special connection and familiarity that we cannot explain. If I had your faith, I would know it was just meant to be. Where I am, I just accept without asking why. I am trying to take the approach now of trying to be more responsive to other forces in my life. I feel our meetings was as one of those events and I am grateful for it. Time will reveal the outcome. Maybe I will find that peace. Donna will enjoy reading this. Thank You.

ROB AND JACOBA

Rob was the brilliant Dutch scientist who wrote the book PREPARED TO ANSWER. He was working for a Dutch company and was called back to Holland. He chose to stay in the US and bought acreage in Hidden Valley near Quilcene. Washington. He had a wife who was Christian and kept nagging him about coming to church. He had time now to do some research on why he thought it was a dumb idea. By the time he finished his research, he turned from an atheist to believer, and felt the call to tell his story. He joined the little church in Quilcene and offered to give a talk to any who were interested in his book just off the press. Lou and I went every Sunday for that important hour for nearly a year and mostly challenged each topic. For example, Noah and the great flood. Where did all that water come from and how did a man build a boat that would withstand tumultuous storms that would be held together by the tree sap and twine that was available in those days. How could he and his family spend years without an income source to support his family and secure the materials needed to build. Then there was the animal collection, the waste disposal, the food source, and separating the predators from the prey, etc.

We explored how this could have happened and discussed the probabilities that Noah may have been a wealthy merchant that had a fleet of boats that sailed up and down the Euphrates and the Tigris River carrying food, wine, animals, supplies, needed materials and resources for survival.

When the floods came, he could link up his barges with the strong twine available, put one on top of the other for separating the food from the animals, predators from the prey, waste disposal and ventilation opportunities. All the water could have come from a giant asteroid smashing into the earth that caused a giant tsunami that spread across a world that did show evidence of a great flood at some time in its history.

I used to get ready to meet Rob on Sundays by researching. My tipping point was the Shroud of Turin. I was glued for one full week to recordings from an international conference of scientists held on March of 2010 at the Ohio State University. The big one for me was the image on the burial cloth of Jesus that was viewed by many as having been painted on. The cloth is rarely available for the public to view. One scientist took pictures of the image and was amazed when he developed it, in that the image was actually a photographic negative that when printed out turned into an actual face. Photography was certainly not a factor in those early days. The bible states that when Mary Magdalen entered the tomb of Jesus, she found the shroud was "empty", not "unfolded."

People are composed of matter in motion, vibrating at an intensity that light does not pass through. If this matter is sped up and the particles separate into their anatomic parts, these particles could pass through material like a shroud (and cave entrances and even doors). If this was a supernatural event, the HE was who HE said HE was, and what HE said makes all the difference.

It was during those days with Rob that I turned from a casual Christian to a believer. I have always been grateful to Rob for the change in my life for the peace that comes from being a Christian.

When Rob's wife had a massive stroke last year, I was heartened to see Rob spend full time on giving Jacoba his total attention to her healing. He gave weekly reports on their amazing progress which was beyond the norm for the severity of her stroke. They were stuck on limitation by the nerve pain in her shoulder caused by the very weak muscles not being able to hold the arm in the socket. The nerves were injured by the stretching and the foot nerve injury by pressure of the leg bracing.

I knew that I was coming to Washington State for the summer, and that as a retired physical therapist that had a piece of equipment that I took with me when I left my practice that treated nerve pain. I would take this machine and have the privilege to use it to help these good friends. Long story short, the machine helped the shoulder, but not the leg nerve injury. I do know that peripheral nerve injuries heal at a rate of an inch a month on average because peripheral nerves have a myelin sheath to transverse regenerating nerves in contrast to the central nervous system that does not.

Rob went to his computer to learn all about the why and how this machine worked, and I taught him what to do and why. I then left the machine at their house for the summer. We also spent some time at the pool at the marina doing reciprocal motion and general pain free ranges of motion. I remember the day we had Jacoba floating on her back supported by a noodle and kicking her legs alternately for independent propulsion. She looked at me and said, "I love you Ruth". I cannot tell you the joy I felt to be able to give some comfort to these two worthy people. Wish I could have been a complete help, but Rob wrote that he bought his own machine to continue after I collected my machine at the end of the summer when I flew back to Florida after the summer on the boat.

Subsequent messages from Rob have been detail questions about the best use of his new machine and the possibility of a Florida visit to investigate a more suitable living situation for keeping Coba functioning. I am delighted to think that I can be of further service to these wonderful children of God. This would be such a joy, I am excited just thinking about the possibilities.

THE JOBS GOT MORE CHALLENGING AS I WENT ALONG

ERIC

Eric was our first born. From his early teens, without any guidance from either Lou or I, he was a prayer warrior for Jesus. He was captain of the football team and senior class president. He carried a bible in his backpack and it became an "in" thing to do at Jefferson High School. He graduated from Washington State College in electrical engineering and as ROTC honor graduate, He got to choose his military path and chose pilot training. He went on to graduate from test pilot school a short time later, added some graduate degrees and was a professor of Astronautics at the United States Airforce Academy. His brother Steve was teaching electrical engineering at the same time at the Academy, and they felt it was their mission to mentor students who were in trouble because this country needed Godly leaders.

He married a pastor's daughter and spent his life connected to a church. He retired as a Colonel after 23 years of a stellar career as lead engineer on the F15 aircraft, liaison for the air force at the pentagon, later liaison for the air force on the joint strike fighter with the Boeing Company and post military with a top security company in space research and then his own company when he contracted Lyme Disease. He went undiagnosed during his physical struggles of fatigue and brain fog. During a top security meeting he met a man from his church and asked him to pray for him as he as feeling suicidal. The man reported him to the FBI and the CIA. They came and took his computer, his cellphone, raided his apartment, and put him in a mental institution under suicide watch, medicated and in restraints.

Eric lost his security clearance, his contracts, and the work he loved to do. With a 4-year messy divorce, with each hearing cancelled because of contesting just before a hearing adding another 6 months delay. He became more depressed with ruminating suicidal thoughts. His motivation for not killing himself was his fear of meeting God on the other side and being told that he had not been a good and faithful servant.

I am blessed with good health and make a yearly visit to my physician. Daughter Kris was visiting during this visit, so she joined me. The doctor walked into the room and asked, "Well Ruth, how are you?". I answered, "my replications are slowing down, and my telomeres are disappearing". Kris thought that was funny and sent me a book for Mother's Day called "The Telomere Effect". I wanted to read it and give her a report to let her know how much I appreciated it.

Before leaving, I had a phone call from Ann, Eric's fiancée, who has been ministering to Eric during his depression. Ann related that his comment to anything was that he did not want to live any more. She was glad that I was coming for the summer and said she needed a LOT of help. I remember my conversation with God on that day was, "God, this job is bigger than I am, I am going to need a LOT of help with this one". I actually wept with the enormity of this task and begged for HIS guidance.

I got on the airplane, and knowing I had a 6-hour flight, I began to read my book, "The Telomere Effect". During the first hour, I found myself underlining in red some very important passages that would help Eric. Some were key words and others were entire paragraphs that were worth of note. By the second hour there were so many notations that I had to stop. It occurred to me that THIS was God talking to me. Where else could I get so much information in a form that I could readily use for my purpose of helping Eric.

Daughter Lori picked me up at the airport and I spent the night at their house. I sat down at their computer and typed then printed out all the notations underlined in red for Eric. The following is the paper I printed out and reviewed with Eric and Ann the following day for over an hour.

Eric:

When your father died over a year ago, I honestly felt HIS unmistakable presence for one entire week in multiple ways. Prior to his death, I always assumed my job was family oriented. Since his death, my job has been to be used in HIS service. I never again felt HIS presence UNTIL YESTERDAY on the airplane coming to Seattle. I knew that I had a real challenge of service to HIM on your behalf. I felt overwhelmed at the enormity of this job of service to my own family. I prayed in tears for God to give me the wisdom to do HIS work on your behalf. I felt so inadequate and unworthy.

On Mother's Day Kris sent me a book called "The Telomere Effect". I was reading it on the flight to Seattle and found some great points that related to you. I underlined them in red. About an hour into the flight, I had so many pages and paragraphs highlighted that were pertinent to your quandary that by the second hour into the fight it became clear to me that this was God answering my prayers for HIS help, giving me words I could say to you in a form I could readily access to bring you back into the world of the living and productivity. The following are some of the quotes from the book that I began to underline in red as relevant, powerful, and memorable. This was my answer to my prayers and fervent plea for HIS guidance. It is my inspired attempt to help you through this rough patch in your life and again find joy in all the wonderful attributes I know you have deep in your soul.

1. Telomeres are the capping structures at the end of your DNA that makes up your chromosomes. They do not simply carry out commands issued by your genetic code but are listening to you. They absorb the instructions that you give them. Thinking makes it so. They contribute to your mood, speed of aging, your risk of degenerative disease. We can change the way we age at the most elemental level. Each time you say you want to die, you are closer to doing just that.

2. Feeling threatened is not the only way to respond to stress. It is also to feel a sense of challenge. People with a challenge response may feel anxious but also may feel excited and energized. They have a "bring it on" mentality. Whereas the threat response prepares you to shut down and tolerate the pain, the challenge response helps you muster your resources.

3. Successful folks have a history of seeing their life problems as challenges to be surmounted, creating the psychological and physiological condition for you to engage fully, perform at our best, and win. The threat response is characterized by withdrawal and defeat as you slump in your seat or freeze your body preparing for wounding and shame as you anticipate a bad outcome. What does

this mean for you? It means you have reason to be hopeful. We do not mean to underestimate the potential that very difficult or intractable situations have for harm, but you can help protect your telomeres by shifting the way you view those events. Can you learn to feel challenge instead? Research says the answer is yes. We are largely unaware of the mental chatter in our minds and it's effect on us. Certain thought patterns appear to be unhealthy. These include the suppression and rumination as well as the negative thinking that characterizes hostility and pessimism. We can't totally change our automatic responses. You can choose to feel the challenge and think positive. (Threat-shrink, challenge-energize) Some of us are born ruminators or pessimist, but we can learn how to keep those automatic patterns from hurting us and even find humor in them. Learning about your style of thinking can be surprising and empowering. Rumination is the act of rehashing your problems over and over. It is seductive. Being caught in rumination is more like getting sucked into a whirlpool that hurtles you increasingly negative, self-destructive thoughts. When you ruminate, you are less actually effective at solving problems and you feel much worse.

4.   The purpose of life is not to be happy, but to matter, to be productive, to be useful, to have it make some difference that you have lived at all. It does not have to be a competition between being happy and being productive with purpose, they come together. A strong sense of our values and purpose can serve as a bedrock foundation that helps us feel stability throughout life.

5.   Another technique for resilient thinking is self-compassion. Self-compassion is nothing more than kindness toward yourself, the knowledge that you are not alone in your suffering, and the ability to turn around and face difficult emotions without getting lost in them. Instead of beating yourself up, you treat yourself with the same warmth and understanding you would extend to a friend.

6.   The Dali Lama wakes up every day and says, "I am fortunate to be alive. I have a precious human life. I am not going to waste it. Start your day with gratitude.

7.   Extreme emotional states have an effect on your cell aging machinery, telomeres, microconidia, and inflammatory processes.

When depressed, one feels as if he has no future, feels overwhelmed, and even physically painful. More than 350 million worldwide suffer from it. The good news is that there are successful medications that when properly administered bring a successful outcome.

8. Dr, Elizabeth Kubler Ross says, "The most successful people we have known are those that have known defeat, known suffering, and have found their way out of the depths. These people have an appreciation, a sensitivity, an understanding of life that fills them with compassion, gentleness, and a deep and loving concern. Beautiful people do not just happen.

9. The breathing break is a way to keep negative emotions from living past their natural life span. You can make it a habit, so it helps you at any time, not just during hard times. Mind clearing, practice in choosing what it is you wish to accept and have some success at those choices.

10. The problem with avoiding whatever is making you anxious is that the avoidance actually perpetuates the feelings of anxiety. You avoid the things you want and need to do, and never learn it is possible to tolerate the discomfort. Your life becomes smaller and smaller, more and more tense, those anxious feelings blown into full grown clinical disorder that interferes with your life. With loving support available to you, your proper medical supervision, discipline on your part, and a reminder that you are not alone. You are loved by many who stand by your side. Today is the day we begin anew for a better tomorrow.

Much love, Mom

The Telomere Effect, Elizabeth Blackburn PH. D, Elissa Epel, PH. D., DeWard Publishing, 2010, pgs. 63-66.

Eric in his search for healing had been to the Amen Clinic in Bellevue, WA., and had a workup that included extensive brain scans and blood work to determine his diagnosis. Ann and I decided that at this juncture, he needed more medical help than he was getting leaving him in limbo. We set up an appointment and told him that we were taking him to Amen Clinic. We were surprised at his negative reaction that included initial refusal to participate until we prevailed. There was a 3-day intensive work up with the 3rd day a visit with the physician.

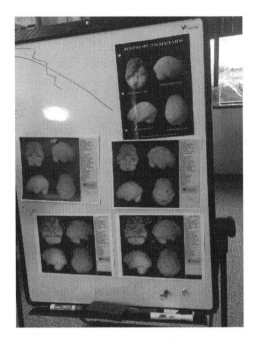

Never in this lifetime have I seen such evidence that "ANTS" (automatic negative thinking sustained) can cause actual physical changes in the brain that are measurable. The scan from the Amen Clinic above is a picture of a normal brain on the top row. The second row is that of Eric's brain in 2012. The third row is that of Eric's brain in June 2018. Actual physical destruction in the frontal lobe is so unmistakably clear. The doctor gave the cause for this destruction as ruminations or the constant automatic negative thinking that insures that the body reflect in physical measures that thinking makes it so.

This same doctor also gave a list of things that Eric can do to alter the physical changes seen above. Positive changes can be just as measurable.

1. Nutrition from food, nutraceutical/ supplements
2. Regular aerobic exercises
3. Gratitude practice, keep a log of the things for which you are grateful
4. Deep relaxation, hand warming technique, diaphragmatic breathing practice in choosing what it is you wish to think and have some success at those choices.
5. Cognitive behavioral therapy
6. Men's small groups

7. Brain games
8. Healthy support circle
9. Meaningful endeavors
10. Make a contract with yourself. Journal what you are feeling, sensing, what is working, your adult spiritual purpose plan. Stop and figure out what you want your life to look like, what is most important to you going forward, your mission or calling, a deep sense of purpose.
11. Recommended reading
12. Surround yourself with positive people

Other people can pray, wish for support, work toward etc. to help but the hard work is to be done by Eric. Great people never came from an easy past as we know that the struggle makes you strong. Negative thinking is the work of Lucifer, do not let him win.

This is the time to move forward, practice the discipline and purpose driven efforts to make the changes for the life this open to you with focus and determination.

We had subsequent meetings with Eric over the summer and each one accompanied by attempts to support his positive path forward. Examples include my philosophy of life that works for me.

GPS Survivor skills

Based on physiological principles, it is the free-flowing energy going into and out of a living cell that keeps this cell nourished and healthy. When energy goes out of a cell and is blocked, say by anger in all of its forms, the cost to the body is inflammatory. When energy is blocked by coming into a cell, say by fear in all its forms, the cost is degenerative for lack of nutrient.

The best buildings are erected and maintained by design and a plan to keep it functioning at high levels. The following is my design and plan to stay healthy and it works for me. As my doctor says, "you are already beyond life expectancy. I should be asking how you do it in place of me telling you what to do.

There are 6 principles that I use when life becomes challenging.

1. When you are feeling stressed or down, go out and do something for someone quick. This is energy out, but more important, by thinking beyond you own miserable current circumstances, you diminish your misery because you are changing focus.
2. Do something for yourself. You need to put energy in to continue putting out. It is OK to pamper yourself with your favorite pleasure, like going out going out to lunch or dinner with friends, go to a movie, read a book, have a manicure or a massage.
3. Produce something. This could be writing a letter or a book, compose a song, paint a picture, make a garden. This is energy out.
4. Learn something. Read a book, play the piano, attend a lecture. This is energy in.
5. Love something. This can be a person, a cat or dog, flowers, beautiful sunset. This is energy out.
6. Let someone love you. This is probably the hardest part, because it makes you vulnerable. This is energy in.

Putting this all together, you have doing something for someone or for you is for the body.

Learning or producing something is for the mind.

Love something or let someone love you is for the spirit. Putting it all together covers all the bases of Body, Mind, and Spirit. It seems to leave little room for misery.

Summary

I write this book in the hope that by doing so I can bring peace to the lives of other men and women who are or will be going through the loss of a life partner. My path was blessed by the unmistakable presence of my God for most of one week of my husband's passing. I knew HIS peace and will be eternally grateful for his presence. I have felt that I may be delusional, but if this is the dream, I am still living the dream a year and a half later.

While I was on the boat in WA. State this summer, I got notices from my Florida neighbors that 3 of my friend's husbands had died in the past 3 months. I miss my husband and am totally aware of the stark difference in this life without him, but feel blessed to have been given the opportunity to escape the feelings of depression, of feeling lost or full of self-pity, of days of pit of the stomach emptiness and despair.

The peace of being a Christian and the trust in HIS guidance, coming alive in the faith, submitting to HIS leadership, and making my life going forward being used in HIS service makes life after Lou so different, yet so satisfying that there is no room for wandering in the darkness and despair. Becoming aware of the nudges that arise alerting one to what you can offer in HIS service takes precedence over mindless fun-loving adventures, keep in mind that you can enjoy these too when there is not a job to do.

At 90 years of age, I love life and living. I look forward to many more and will be just as happy to move on to the next life when that time comes. It is my hope that these remarks will ease the pain with the many suggestions and references given in these chapters that are useful and worthy of your time in reading them.

Ruth DiDomenico, November 16 2018

References

1. Rob VanDeWeghe, Prepared to Answer, a Guide to Christian Evidences, DeWard Publishing, 2010
2. Elizbeth Blackburn, PH D, Elissa Epel, PH D, The Telomere Effect, living younger, healthier, longer, Grand Central Publishing, 2017.
3. Daniel G. Amen, MD, Tania Amen, BSN, The Brain Warrior's Way, Penguin, Random House, 2016.

About The Author

BS Degree
> Eastern Michigan University,

MS Degree,
> Neuroanatomy/physiology, University of Colorado.

Lt. US Army Medical Specialist Corp, Korean War,

Assoc. Professor Health Science Dept., University of WA.

Owner/Administrator Rehabilitation Agency and private physical therapy practice 35 years.

Married to Louis DiDomenico 62 years, 6 children, 20 grandchildren currently living in the Villages, Florida.

Printed in the United States
By Bookmasters